Croutons on a Cow Pie

by Baxter Black

illustrated by Don Gill and Bob Black

COYOTE COWBOY COMPANY
RECORD STOCKMAN PRESS

Denver 1988

All poems written by Baxter Black

Copyright© 1988 by Baxter Black

Published by   Coyote Cowboy Company
Record Stockman Press
P.O. Box 1209
Wheat Ridge, Colorado 80034

LIBRARY OF CONGRESS CATALOGING IN PUBLICATION DATA
Main entry under:
Cowboy Poetry

Bibliography: p
1. Coyote Cowboy Poetry
2. Cowboys–Poetry
3. Poetry–Cowboy
4. Humor–Cowboy
5. Agriculture–Poetic Comment

I. Black, Baxter, 1945–

Library of Congress #88-071575
ISBN 0-939343-03-7

OTHER BOOKS BY BAXTER
THE COWBOY AND HIS DOG ©1980
A RIDER, A ROPER AND A HECK'UVA WINDMILL MAN ©1982
ON THE EDGE OF COMMON SENSE, THE BEST SO FAR ©1983
DOC, WHILE YER HERE ©1984
BUCKAROO HISTORY ©1985
COYOTE COWBOY POETRY © 1986

TABLE OF CONTENTS

DRESSIN' UP

Dressin' up to certain good folks
Might mean a suit and a tie
Designer socks, a diamond ring
Or hair like the fourth of July!

    But out where we make a livin'
    Tennis shoes don't fit the bill.
    They don't set too good in a stirrup
    I reckon they never will.

We're more into spurs, hats and leggin's
'Cause punchin' cows ain't all romance
But cowboys clean up on occasion
For weddings, a funeral or dance.

    The dress code for everyday cowboys
    Ain't changed since Grandpa got wise,
    A good pair of boots, yer Sunday hat
    And yer newest pair of levi's.

Besides, deckin' a cowboy out
In street shoes, a suit and a tie
Would make as good an impression
As croutons on a cow pie.

A HUNDRED YEARS TOO LATE

I psychoanalyzed myself
And pondered at my fate.
And realized that I was born
A hundred years too late.

A cowpoke in this day and age
Must learn to specialize.
The fact I'm barely gettin' by
Should come as no surprise.

There was a time when you could tell
A top hand by his hat.
But knowin' cows is not enough,
Geneticists do that!

Once, every puncher worth his salt
Could rope a wild steer.
Now motel cowboys do that trick
At Cheyenne every year.

I might have been a bunkhouse bard
A hundred years ago,
But modern cowboy poets star
On Johnny Carson's show.

Somehow I think if I had lived
When horses reigned supreme
I'd carved my niche in history,
At least that's what I dream.

I'd built my reputation with
Each buckin' bronc I spurred.
My daring exploits would have made
My name a household word.

Amongst the cowboys of today
I'm just an average Joe.
I could have made more of myself
A hundred years ago.

If only fortune would have smiled
And laid my egg back then,
I'd been a bigger fish, for sure,
Instead of ridin' pens.

But I guess I should be thankful
In spite of what I've said.
If I'd been born that long ago
Then right now I'd be dead!

THE ACCIDENT

My ol' friend Wayne had an accident
Seems he'd treated himself to a nip
And came home late with the bottle stashed
In the pocket there on his right hip.

He fumbled around for the house key
'Cause his wife habitually locked it,
Pushed open the door, slipped on the rug
And the bottle broke in his pocket!

He bit his tongue to stifle a scream!
He could feel the pieces of glass
As they cut through his pants and underwear
Carving X's and O's on his *

He raced to the bathroom to check it
And proceeded to make his repairs,
Depleting the entire first aid kit.
Then he quietly slipped up the stairs.

Next morning he slept like a baby
'Til his wife, who was loud as Big Ben,
Shattered his peaceful dreams by saying,
"So, you came home last night drunk again!"

"But, Dear, I . . . I thought you were sleeping?"
"Yes, I was, but it's perfectly clear,
I just came up from the downstairs throne
And there's band aids all over the mirror!"

THE ELK HUNT

Lo, the weary hunter came
    No blood upon his hands.
His darlin' wife, in sweet relief
    Bid welcome to her man.

For ten long days he'd hunted
    From ridge to rocky stream
With sportsmen cronies like himself
    Alas, no elk was seen.

He told her how at daybreak
    They'd light out from the camp
And walk until their back and legs
    Were knotted in a cramp.

Then how around the campfire
    With reverence they would speak
About their wives and families
    Their plans for Holy Week,

Of politics and healthfood
    Of hunting as a sport,
Then just for therapeutic sake
    They'd have a little snort!

She bore his epic saga
    As wives are forced to bear
But winced when he said she forgot
    To pack his underwear.

She stilled the mighty hunter
    Her answer left him stunned,
"You must have overlooked them, dear,
    I packed'em with your gun!"

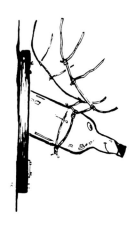

COWBOY HEAVEN

I never did do it for the money
I guess you done figgered that out
But I's never broke, fer long anyways
Gettin' rich ain't what it's about

    Gettin' high on the smell of a sunrise
    A'horseback, a long way from camp
    Or the sound of the crickets competin'
    With a hissin' kerosene lamp

That's reason enough to be out here, that . . .
And livin' my life nearly free
'Cause I ain't punchin' cows fer the payday
It means more than money to me

    If I could I'd stay on here forever
    Without meanin' no disrespect
    To the folks sellin' box seats in Glory
    And passin' the plate to collect

Somewhere inside me they say there's a soul
Just waitin' to fly when I croak
And I'd sure be a bit disappointed
If Heaven was only a joke

    And I'm ready to go, if I have to
    Though I plan on wearin' my hat
    But I hope it's as good as they claim it
    'Cause it's hard to beat where I'm at

Some believers have reached the conclusion
That men get recycled like cans
And eventually wind up in Heaven
After wearin' numerous brands

    If that's true, then my soul prob'ly lit here
    By chance, on a wing and a prayer
    Which explains why it's so much like Heaven
    'Cause maybe I'm already there

ON THE EDGE OF COMMON SENSE

Baxter Black DVM

by Boller

Hi frendz and felo cowdogz, I, Baxter's faythfull unaprizeated 'good dog' and bezt frend, have subsutooted my collum for his. Becase he takes grate delite in piken on mans best frend, us, the all Amerakin cowdog. I cannt tell yoo how much monny he haz made riding on hour name..."Go git In The Pikup, Yoo..." Ha, ha, funny as a pech pite in the Gravy Trane!

Lemme tell yoo, I hang out with thes trkey and he is not the cowboy he clamz. The onely whay he can rop a hefer is buy chacing her so long, she falls from egzoshchon. He likes to make okayzhenal refrens to his veteranary skills. Hour ranch iz the onely plase I no that has les than ten cows and the rendering truk stops evreday!

The real seekret to the sekses of hour cattel opperashon is me, ofe corse! Do yoo think a cowboy cood fined a cow in the brush with out uz? Are yoo cedden! Thay ride a long like thay no where ther going but we no there just foloing us.

Thay acte like ther doen uz a faver buy letten us ride into towen. Ther just to laze to clen the junk outa the pikup bed. So we gota sit and garde it while pate each outher on the back at the coffe shop.

All for what? Stak bones and cavear? Rong, bisket lips! Yoo ever eat Coop dog food? It tasts like chiken and gives me gas.

Its time we stood on all fors and be cownted! We perform many vitel servesess on the ranch but Bumbling Black had the awdasety to tell a reporter I wus a prop! I wood like yoo to send me fotografik evadens of uz doing hour doote. Sort of "Cow Dogs in Akshon." Sports Elastrated mite even do a pese on uz. Male yore foto to:

Boller
% Cowdog Hall of Champenz
box 190
Brighten, CO 80601

footnote: Baxter writes a weekly column. A while back his dog, Boller, intercepted the mail and substituted his own column. Boller received many letters from cowdogs sympathetic to his plight. Needless to say, he lost them all.

14

KARL'S FIRST SALE

Anybody that has ever put on their own livestock sale knows Murphy's Law. Lew and Benny hired on to help Karl make his first purebred offering a success. Karl (that's Karl with a K) was a good cowman who did things the old way. Hard work was all he knew. Lew claimed he was the toughest man he ever met. He was oblivious to pain. He was that rare combination of brute strength and awkwardness. He didn't understand the fine points of creative financing or investor counselling. His neighbors even suggested that Karl was a little stupid. They were still sayin' it after their banks had foreclosed and they were doin' day work for Karl!

The day before the sale, it rained . . . and rained. They got the sale ring panels up, built the auction box and bleachers, and rented Porta Potties. They washed cattle, borrowed coffee makers, printed programs, bought ketchup, raked gravel and re-inforced the loading chute.

"Now, boys," says Karl, "I like my cattle worked gentle and easy. No chousin'em. No need to cowboy here. Saddle up and follow me. We'll gather the bulls from across the road."

As the bulls came outta the timber, they began to drift toward a fresh plowed field. They were frisky, kickin' up a little. Karl thought they were makin' a break for it. . . He panicked! "Stop'em, boys!" Karl charged the herd like Santa Anna takin' the Alamo! The bulls scattered into the knee deep mud like frightened quail! Karl raced across the field to head'em off. His horse shot through the open gate. A two-inch wide homemade strap-iron gate hinge reached out and tore a 15-stitch piece outta Karl's right ear. Never phased him!

Lew took a break from rewashin' the bulls. He heard poundin' and walked into the barn. Karl had his 17 foot extension ladder leaned against a 2x4 beam up in the ceiling. Lew and Benny had nailed the beam lightly to the roof trusses from the bottom. The nails were heads down. Karl was hammerin' a light fixture into the top of the beam with all his might. Every resounding 'thwack' separated the beam further from the trusses. Karl was directly above Lew's Spring-O-Matic tilt table. The Spring-O-Matic had vertical pipes that stuck up like bamboo spears in a tiger trap.

Just as Lew raised a warning finger, a final hammer blow knocked the beam free. Beam, hammer, ladder, light fixture, bird's nest and Karl, plummeted into the Spring-O-Matic! When he rose from the wreckage, it looked like somebody had done a wheelie on his forehead!

Benny had jack knifed the silage wagon in the main entrance of the sale barn the night before, for easy access. "Let's git that outta the way!" said Karl. He jumped up in the tractor seat, jammed the ol' Farmall in 4th HIGH, blew the dust outta the exhaust and popped the clutch! He dumped 4 tons of chopped straw in the doorway! The wind picked it up and piled it in Dakota drifts over the bleachers.

Sale day was crisp and cold. At Karl's suggestion, Lew and Benny drug a big smudge pot into the crowded sale barn. They lit it and turned it on "high." As long as it burned full blast, it didn't smoke, but it sure put out the heat. Bidders were down to their tee shirts when the fuel finally ran out and it began to smoke. A black cloud settled over the straw-covered crowd.

Lew hooked a chain around the sizzling, smoking pot and pulled it out into the road. He went back to the cattle and worked until he heard the explosion. Rushing around the barn, he saw Karl laying flat on his back. His arms and legs were spread out like he was makin' gravel angels. His hat was blown off and the front of his shirt looked like a barbecue grill. Lew thought he was dead.

The smudge pot had disappeared. Apparently Karl had gone out to refill the smudge pot with diesel. When he poured the fuel into the red-hot metal, it created fumes which ignited and turned the pot into a grenade! His wife covered Karl's face with Unguntine. His hat looked like he'd worn it to welding practice and he couldn't hear very well.

Back in the sale barn, the action began to heat up. Don was the ring man. He'd backed up behind the corner of the auction box, because the bull that was sellin' was on the fight. Karl was settin' in the auction box intently watching the crowd. He was absent-mindedly switchin' the bull's nose with his whip popper. The bull began to shake and twitch. The more Karl diddled, the madder he got. He charged the auction box and lifted it three feet off the ground! The auctioneer fell backwards, spurs up, right outta the cockpit! Karl pitched forward into the sale ring.

The bull had him down and was grinding him into sawdust. Don grabbed a metal folding chair and swung it at the bull. The bull swerved at the last second and Don blindsided Karl upside the head! Cold-cocked him! Karl fell like a bag of loose salt. There was a gash between his eyebrows and his other ear looked like a gutted salmon! To this day Karl thinks it was the bull that got'im. Don's never told him different.

Benny walked up to Lew who was standin' in the sale ring door surveying the battlefield. "Sorry I got you into this, Benny. A man should get hazard pay workin' for Karl."

"Shoot," said Benny, "I'll work here next year for nothin' just to see what happens!"

THE PHONE CALL

It's always been a mys'try
In the winter when it's slow
Why a rancher gets up early
When he's got no place to go!

> He prowls around the kitchen
> Like a burglar on parole
> In his air conditioned slippers
> With the toe there in the hole.

Then he builds a pot of coffee
And has a little cup
'Til he thinks of some good reason
To wake somebody up!

> And all around the valley
> Folks are nestled in their bed
> Unaware an egg is hatching
> In the rancher's little head.

He's reread the livestock paper
Since getting up alone
But he's still not quite decided
Just who he's gonna phone!

> The assistant county agent?
> The forest ranger's boss?
> The banker? brand inspector?
> The commissioner that lost?

The vet? The Co-op salesman,
Though he can't recall his name,
But it really doesn't matter
'Cause anybody's game.

> He quivers like a panther
> About to pounce his prey
> As the innocent lay sleeping
> Just a dial tone away.

By daylight it's all over
And he's reached a fever pitch!
The way he's stompin' 'round the house
His wife is wond'rin' which

> Potential victim got the call
> And had his brain massaged
> With the lecture, she, just yesterday,
> Herself, had tried to dodge!

But little does she realize
Just why he's in a tizzy,
See, his neighbors got up earlier . . .
And all the lines were busy!

ALL BEEF NUGGETS

In the last twenty years there's been a significant trend toward larger cattle. Purebred breeders have concentrated their exotic genes 'til the modern bovine looks like a Great Dane on steroids. Our cattle have gotten bigger and bigger and bigger! It's gotten to the point where the Chianina people don't have to hire short Italians anymore to take that picture! But I'm wondering if maybe we're goin' the wrong way?

Maybe we should be breeding our cattle smaller and smaller and smaller...I'm talkin' BITE SIZE! Something that would fit in a hot hog bun, on a fondue stick! Convenience food.

Think how it would revolutionize our business. As producers, we wouldn't have to own all that land. We could give it back to the government. Turn everything into a prairie dog park. We could move into town, buy a nice house and turn our critters out in the back yard.

At branding time you wouldn't even have to furnish the banker with a horse. If he wants to count the cows just give him a grocery bag and point him out the back door. If you were cuttin' the bull calves you'd just reach into the grocery bag, pull out the calf, hold him in the palm of your hand and use your fingernail clippers!

And how 'bout hauling cattle? Look at their feet, cowboys, they were not meant to be off the ground! Nowhere in the Bible does it mention semi load! Say you wanted to haul your new mini-cattle to the sale or the stockshow. You'd just put'em in the back deck of the family car and go down the road. "Well, Mother, it's time to feed and water the stock." You whip into a Denny's, gather'em up and turn'em loose in the salad bar!

We'd put packin' houses outta business. Just clean'em like a blue gill! Peel the hide off and eat'em bone in! All beef nuggets!

There are some cowmen who have spent a lifetime improving their herd through genetic selection. They have made prodigious use of artificial insemination. There are actually people in our industry who have made a living artificially inseminating other people's cows. They are thinking to themselves as they read this, "Wait a minute! I can barely hit that deal the way it is now and you want me to...!" But   I've got their problem solved too. Just dip'em in it!

And finally, the   greatest advantage of all is one we don't even   think about. I read in the Wall Street Journal   that folks are makin' a killin' today   in microchips!

20

THE #2 HAIRBALL

Ever buy one of those feeders
    That never seems to get well?
Right off the truck to the sick pen
    Straight from receiving to hell!

They're common. Each semi load's got one
    'Specially if they're from a sale.
I call'em a Number 2 Hairball,
    They're fluffy, but thin as a rail.

They look like those two day old cornflakes
    That stick to the side of the bowl.
Pot bellied, wormy and drippin'
    From every unplugable hole.

His muzzle's as wide as a suitcase,
    His tail comes down to his heels,
His hide's as dry as a Baptist bar,
    The last brand still hasn't peeled!

You treat'em for weeks with your potions
    With everything Doc recommends
But sixty days later he still gets his mail
    Addressed to the hospital pen.

Where do these chronics all come from?
    I've had some time to reflect.
There's a purebred herd of'em somewhere . . .
    At least that's what I suspect.

A place where animal science
    And Doctor Frankenstein meet.
Where the characteristics they breed for
    Are the same ones you try to treat!

Like, only one lung ever works right.
    The cough's just part of the deal
And scours is standard equipment
    Plus the footrot that never will heal.

No matter which treatment you try out
    You're confused at every attempt.
'Cause one hundred four point seven
    Is really their normal temp!

So you keep pumpin' medicine in'em
    'Til the drug bill is high as the sky
Yet they never completely recover
    But the bloody buggars won't die!

Now, of course, I'm makin' this all up.
    No chronic cow breeder's been caught.
But if I was a medicine maker . . .
    I just might give it some thought.

THE HIRED MAN

When they put him on the payroll
All the cowboys wondered "why?"
'Cause he didn't own a saddle,
Couldn't rope and didn't try!

So they gave him all the bad jobs,
The ones that they'd put off
And went about their business
Leavin' him to clean the trough

And irrigate. To fix the fence
And chop the thistle down
And when they all ran out of beer
Was him that went to town.

He handled all the details
The cowboys would ignore
That held the place together
Kept the wolves back from the door.

They only saw him now and then,
At night when they'd come in
'Cause things were runnin' awful smooth
And they were busy men.

Nobody ever noticed
That he always did his part
Until the day the windmill froze
And the pickup wouldn't start!

The coyotes got the chickens
And the butane tank went dry.
The milk cow tore the barn down,
The mechanic's wife got high!

Nobody'd stoked the wood stove
Or started up a fire
So the cook refused'em breakfast
And threatened to retire!

The dogs tore up the smoke house
Like they'd hit it with a bomb!
The ranch ground to a stand still!
And the cowboys said, "Where's Tom?"

Seems, they never really thought about
How much they'd miss his face . . .
It finally hit'em on the day
The hired man quit the place!

GOOD BYE, OLD MAN

Somewhere deep in the old man's eyes
A mem'ry took a hold.
It fought the ageless undertow
That drains and mocks the old.

I wiped a dribble off his chin
"Pop, tell me what you see?"
"It's all the boys I rode with,
I think they've come for me."

Unconsciously I checked the door,
"It's nothin' but the wind.
You better try and git some rest,
Tomorrow we'll go in."

"Is that you, Bob? I can't quite see.
Yer mounted mighty well.
You never rode a horse that good
When we were raisin' hell."

"Lie down, old man. There's no one here."
"No, wait, that looks like Clyde.
He helped me put ol' Blue to sleep.
Why, hell, he even cried.

"Now don't forget to check the salt,
Them cows'll drift back down.
Well I'll be damned, there's Augustine,
He worked here on the Brown

When I hired on to buckaroo . . .
But that's been fifty years."
The old man squinched his rheumy eyes,
I dabbed away the tears.

The boss had told me he was old,
Had seen a lot of springs.
I bet ya if you peeled his bark
You'd count near eighty rings.

We'd rode the last three summers here
Together on the rim.
Just he and I, for puncher's pay.
I'd learned a lot from him.

But now I'm settin' by his bed,
Uncertain what to do.
I ain't too good at nursin' coots.
I'm only twenty-two.

"I reckon that I'm ready now.
My friends are set to go.
They've got an extra mount cut out
That's just for me, I know."

"You've got to stop this foolish talk!
You shouldn't overdo!
Pop, all you need's a good night's sleep,
You'll be as good as new."

"Don't make it complicated, kid,
Cut a pal some slack.
The saddle on that extra horse . . .
That's my ol' weathered kak.

"I'm comin', Bob, I'll be right there."
He winked a misty eye
And tried to reach up for his hat,
Then died without a sigh.

I'll tellya, man, it freaked me out!
I dang near come in two!
I'd never watched a person die,
Especially one I knew.

I tried to say a little prayer
But all I knew was grace.
So I just said, "Good Bye, Old Man"
And covered up his face.

I poured myself the bitter dregs
And stood out on the step.
Alone I listened to the night,
As still as death, except,

I thought I heard above the coffee
Sloshin' in my cup
The far off, easy, pleasured sound
Of old friends catchin' up.

THE OYSTER

The sign upon the cafe wall said OYSTERS: fifty cents.
"How quaint," the blue eyed sweetheart said, with some bewildermence,
"I didn't know they served such fare out here upon the plain?"
"Oh, sure," her cowboy date replied, "We're really quite urbane."

"I would guess they're Chesapeake or Blue Point, don't you think?"
"No m'am, they're mostly Hereford cross . . . and usually they're pink.
But I've been cold, so cold myself, what you say could be true
And if a man looked close enough, their points could sure be blue!"

She said, *"I gather them myself out on the bay alone.
I pluck them from the murky depths and smash them with a stone!"*
The cowboy winced imagining a calf with her beneath
"Me, I use a pocket knife and yank'em with my teeth."

"Oh, my," she said, *"You animal! How crude and unrefined!
Your masculine assertiveness sends shivers up my spine!
But I prefer a butcher knife too dull to really cut.
I wedge it in on either side and crack it like a nut!*

*I pry them out. If they resist, sometimes I use the pliers
Or even Grandpa's pruning shears if that's what it requires!"*
The hair stood on the cowboy's neck. His stomach did a whirl.
He'd never heard such grisly talk, especially from a girl!

"I like them fresh," the sweetheart said and laid her menu down
Then ordered oysters for them both when the waiter came around.
The cowboy smiled gamely, though her words stuck in his craw
But he finally fainted dead away when she said, *"I'll have mine raw!"*

THE MARKER

The very first time I saw him, he was comin' off the truck.
The order buyer had averaged down, or else just plain got stuck!
He went in a pen of feeders but when it came time to sell
The packer buyer cut him off. The reason was plain as hell,

He looked like a long haired Jersey! At least he did to me
And there might have been a camel somewhere in his family tree
'Cause he'd shed his hair in patches, past the point of no return
Sorta like a shaggy carpet that somebody'd tried to burn!

So, he went with tailenders, got sorted off again
And made the rounds when springtime came just goin' from pen to pen.
That summer he went out to grass but he never gained a pound,
We vaccinated him that fall on his second time around.

The weeks drug on but I kept track, in truth he was hard to miss,
'Cause he stuck out like a cold sore on the lips you'd planned to kiss!
One day I told the foreman, "Ya know, ol' Red's been here a while,
I've figgered his performance up and it's time to reconcile."

I had calculated that he'd had six hundred days on feed,
Been through the chute so many times he was almost broke to lead!
He had eaten sixteen thousand pounds of grain since he'd begun
And converted at a ratio of Two-Oh-Two to One.

Which, in fact, is pretty sorry, unless you're raisin' whale,
So, that mornin' in the One-Ton, ol' Red got shipped to the sale.
I was braggin' at the horse barn how I'd prob'ly get a raise
For pointing out that keepin' poor producers seldom pays.

Some of the boys objected, but sentiment has no place
In hard core ag economics. Red was a classical case.
The foreman cut my lecture short that evenin' just about five,
"Git yer butt down to receiving . . . Time for the trucks to arrive."

New cattle were comin' from auctions, local and countrywide.
When I went down to unload'em, I dang near laid down and cried!
Ol' Red come strollin' off the truck like Caesar entering Rome.
He gimme sort of a "Gotcha" look and said "Hi, Honey, I'm Home!"

KEEP ON TRUCKIN'

Horses were meant to be ridden
Chickens were meant to be fried
Fish were meant to be cat food
Pigs were meant to be styed
Sheep were meant to be sweaters
Eagles were meant to be bald
But never, and I mean never, my friend,
Were cattle meant to be hauled!

Nowhere in the Bible does it mention semi load
A trucker sees an ear tag and thinks it's some zip code

No trailer's been invented where cattle fit like spoons
That's why you've never known one that likes Dave Dudley tunes

Fish are sleek and often packed together like sardines
Even kids in schools busses are easy, 'til they're teens

But loadin' cattle in a truck's the very worst, by far
Like stuffin' loose coat hangers in the glove box of your car

A critter's feet are cloven, not meant to be chauffeured
To balance in a trailer, they'd have to perch like birds

They're not equipped with suckers or have prehensile tails
But we shovel in the sawdust and run'em cross the scales

We're proud if we get forty-three crammed on a load of fats
And we don't care if they have to hang upside down like bats

Ever buy your boots too small and stuff'em fulla beans?
Then fill'em up with water to stretch'em at the seams?

The final spoonful sets up like concrete in the toe
Then you have to dig it out like the last calf on the load

In natural surroundings, a steer takes life at ease
When nature calls he pauses and goes where'ere he please

You think it's easy tinklin' whilst speedin' overland?
Just try it from a pickup, standin' up . . . without no hands!

Somehow we think ol' Bossy should admire the truck we bought
But if she had a finger she'd tell us what she thought

So when you see a bovine from your Peterbuilt on high
If she says "Keep on truckin'," she just means "Pass me by!"

TINKER AND LADY

A stranger hangin' around cow workin's, sale barns or gatherin's might get the impression that little love exists between the cowboy and his dog. Only that the dog suffers from verbal abuse or that the cowboy is entitled to sue for mental exasperation. Neither is prone to open displays of affection. The cowboy acts tough and the dog acts bored.

But I remember one time up at the Grouse Creek Ranch. It was in the fall and we were workin' cows. Tinker was the cook. It wasn't that he was a great cook, but he'd always done it and traditions get established regardless of their intrinsic worth. He made a big pot of chili and beans the first night. It was enough to feed the seven of us plus any visiting calvary platoon that might be billeting in the area! After supper we all loaded in the pickup and drove fifteen miles to Pop's ranch.

Pop had a natural hot springs on his place. We bathed and soaked, loaded up and drove back to our ranch. On arrival Tinker realized we'd left his little dog, Lady, back at Pop's. Nobody really worried but Tinker backtracked anyway. The rest of us slept peacefully (the chili and beans was fresh).

Next morning we stumbled into breakfast. The familiar aroma of chili and beans filled the kitchen. Unusual breakfast fare, but nobody said anything. Tinker looked like a dyin' duck in a thunderstorm! He'd been out all night lookin' for Lady.

Tinker was preoccupied all morning. He reheated the chili and beans for lunch. By supper (chili and beans) Tinker had become irritable. He'd walk to the window or outside every few minutes lookin' down the road and whistlin'. That night we slept with the doors and windows open in the bunkhouse.

At breakfast an unpleasant deja vu lay heavy over the table. The chili and beans was the consistency of South Dakota gumbo and smelled like burning brakes. Tinker spoke to no one . . . all day. For supper we had chili and bean sludge. It was the closest I've come to eating lava. The night we slept outside.

Complaining to the cook is bad cowboy etiquette, but we all agreed something had to be done. Had a submarine trained its sonar on our stomachs he'd have thought he was picking up a pod of nauseous killer whales!

Breakfast the third day was fried adobe that tasted vaguely of chili and beans. We ate in silence accompanied by the growling sounds of indigestion and explosive borborygmi. Then we heard the scratching at the door. Tinker jumped up and looked! There was Lady, sore footed, dusty and glad to be home! Tinker picked her up like a baby and hugged her. She licked his face.

Still holding her, he took a big T-bone steak out of the frig and slapped it in the frying pan. After a couple turns he put it on the floor in front of her. She ate all she could and lay down, exhausted. Needless to say, we were happy for them both but we tried to act like it was no big deal so Tinker wouldn't be embarrassed. After he left, we dove the bone!

EAT MORE BEEF!

I'm a fairly frequent victim of the EAT MORE BEEF! campaign.
    I've read the ads and seen the spots intended to explain
That if I will eat real beef, I will be real people
    And have more iron inside me than a rusty army Jeep'll!

It will make me thin and happy and put my life in order
    And I agree in principle, I've been a staunch supporter.
But sometimes all this hoopelah just plain gives me the jitters.
    See, I have a vested interest. I raise the blasted critters!

Which tends to make me cynical, to doubt or even scoff it!
    'Cause from the cowman's point of view, it ain't all fun and profit.
They've crippled more than one good horse and countless good blue heelers,
    An order buyer now and then, plus hordes of wheeler dealers.

And as for me, I've had my share of wounds and lacerations
    Of broken heads and swollen thumbs, unwelcome perforations.
They've knocked me down and knocked me out and overhauled my keister
    And woke me up on Christmas day and kept me up 'til Easter!

They've embarrassed and ignored me, annoyed and misused me.
    They've broke me flat as hammered pie, mistreated and abused me,
And yet I keep on comin' back like bees keep makin' honey.
    Maybe I'm a masochist 'cause it dang sure ain't the money!

So when they tell me EAT MORE BEEF!, I'll try and be attentive.
    But tellin' me's a waste of time, I've got my own incentive.
I've spent a lifetime workin' cows which keeps a man believin.'
    You bet yer life I EAT MORE BEEF! . . . I eat it to get even!

FARMER OR RANCHER?

There is a distinction in the livestock business between ranchers and farmers. But how does a city slicker tell the difference? I have some guidelines that should be helpful.

1. Ranchers live in the west. Except beet growers in Idaho, cotton farmers in Arizona, prune pickers in California and wheat producers in Montana. Farmers live east of Burlington, Colorado. Except for cattle ranchers in the Sandhills of Nebraska, cracker cowboys in Florida, Flinthills cowmen in Kansas, and mink ranchers in Michigan.

2. Farmers wear seed company caps except when they're attending the PCA banquet, the annual cattlemen's meeting or going on a tour to a foreign country. Ranchers wear western hats except when they're roping, putting up hay or feeding cows at 30° below zero.

3. Ranchers wear western boots except when they're irrigating and sleeping. Farmers wear western boots except when they go to town.

4. Farmers work cows afoot, on a tractor, a three wheeler, a motorcycle, in the pickup, snowmobile, road grader, canoe or ultralight. Virtually any motorized contraption except a horse. Ranchers work cows horseback.

5. Farmers can identify grass. Ranchers have trouble distinguishing grass from weeds and indoor-outdoor carpet. Farmers think grass is green. Ranchers think it is yellow.

6. Ranchers haul their dogs around in the pickup and pretend they are stock dogs. Farmers usually leave their pets at home.

7. Farmers think a rope is good for towing farm equipment, tying down bales and staking the milk cow along the highway. A rancher's rope hangs on the saddle and is only used to throw at critters.

8. A rancher wouldn't be caught dead in overalls. A farmer never wears a scarf or spurs.

9. Farmers complain about the weather, the market, the government, the banker, taxes, county roads, the price of seed, equipment, veterinary work, pickups, tires and kids. So do ranchers.

Now that I've made it perfectly clear, let's assume you see a man on Main Street in Enid, Oklahoma. He's wearing western boots, a seed corn cap and has a pocketful of pencils. He's driving his pickup complete with a dog, a saddle and a three wheeler in the back. Which is he, a farmer or rancher?

He's either a rancher on his way to a roping or a farmer coming back from the flea market. The only way to be sure is to examine his rope. If it has more than two knots in it, he's a farmer.

IN DEFENSE OF THE CHICKEN

Everyone says they love chicken,
Ambrosia sent from above.
But nobody loves *a* chicken,
A chicken ain't easy to love.

It's hard to housebreak a chicken.
They just don't make very good pets.
You might teach one bird imitations
But that's 'bout as good as it gets.

Mentally, they're plumb light-headed
And never confused by the facts.
That's why there's no seein' eye chickens,
Guard chickens or trained chicken acts.

And everything tastes like chicken,
From rattlesnake meat to fried bats.
It has anonymous flavor;
I figger they're all Democrats.

Some say this ignoble creature
With his intellect unrefined
And lack of civilized manners
Has little to offer mankind.

But let me suggest, the chicken
Had two contributions to make;
The first was the peckin' order,
The second, the chicken-fried steak!

THE CONSULTANT

Bein' in between jobs ain't no picnic.
In fact, it's downright insultant.
So I printed some cards, put signs in the yard,
And bingo, became a consultant!

I solicited quality rest stops
In search of the right clientele.
Passed out ballpoint pens to all of my friends,
Got an answer machine from Ma Bell.

At last an ol' timer sought my advice.
He brought in his last balance sheet.
I saw with a smile his management style
Was outdated and obsolete.

So I set out to solve all his problems.
I spoke like a preacher possessed.
He sat there amazed, his eyes sorta glazed,
I could see he was truly impressed.

He said not a word as I rambled on.
For effect, I went over it twice.
When time had expired, he politely inquired,
"How much for this expert advice?"

I said, "Fifty bucks." I thought it was fair.
From his looks I thought I could fake it.
But he nodded his head and finally said,
"Well, son, I don't think I'll take it!"

THE FIRST COUNTY AGENT

Clarence of Euphrates was just a simple man
    He graduated ag school from Tigress A&M

It only took him seven days to garner his degree
    But days were longer then, of course, and no one took P.E.

His goals were really modest; to help clean up the air
    To save the world from ignorance, become a millionaire

To always strive for excellence and never be complacent
    So Clarence of Euphrates became a county agent

His first job was a garden, the year was 2 A.S.
    To clarify, that's After Snake, and Eden was a mess!

He organized the fair board though his paperwork was slow
    And told the state director no more than he should know

His achievements in 4-H work were a credit to the kids
    On a field trip to Egypt they built the pyramids

The local folks would cringe in fear and hide out in the thickets
    'Cause everytime that Clarence came, he'd sell'em raffle tickets!

In the Eden County Stockmens he was honored by his peers
    And served as secretary for seven hundred years

He put on endless meetings and countless demonstrations
    With faulty slide projectors and drafty ventilations

He wrote a million pamphlets, read record books galore
    And patted pigs and lambs and kids 'til his hands and heart were sore.

He always judged the apple pies at Eden County Fair
    Although the ancient legends warned of apples, to beware

But Clarence ate'm anyway and scoffed at their reaction
    But alas, he finally died, of apple pie compaction.

COULD BE WORSE

The banker took his ledger out,
The rancher took a seat.
"Let's see, I lent you twenty thou
For cattle, corn and wheat.

"Let's talk about your cattle first."
The rancher's face looked pained.
"You know how bad the market's been,
Lost fifteen," he explained.

"Fifteen what! Fifteen cents a pound?
Fifteen died of thirst?"
"Nope, fifteen thousand dollars lost,
But, hey, it could be worse."

The banker swallowed hard then asked,
"Well, what about your grain?"
"The hoppers ate up all my wheat;
The sweet corn needed rain.

"The pig got sick. My son got drunk
And joined the Moonies' church!
I figger I'm down forty thou
But, hey, it could be worse."

"Whataya mean, 'It could be worse!'
That ain't even funny."
The rancher shrugged and then replied,
*"Could'a been **my** money."*

PILED HIGHER AND DEEPER

Ol' Bubber was cussin' his bad luck
As we watched his bunch crossin' the scale
Which surprised me a bit, 'cause he had to admit
His steers were the best at the sale!

    Weighed eight fifty-two . . . after truckin'!
    Which puzzled me some, I confess
    My quandry, ya see . . . he was neighbors to me
    And mine weighed considerably less!

But still he appeared disappointed.
He spoke as he stared at the floor,
"I can't understand, as hard as I planned
Why them steers didn't weigh a lot more.

    See, A & M put on a meeting
    Extension was all out in force.
    I needed to change how I handled my range
    And they had the answers, of course!

Brush hog the greasewood, burn all the pear,
And fly on the N, P and K
By killin' my weeds and plantin' their seeds
My gains would get better each day.

    Merlin the Nutritionist spoke of
    Ionophores and methanol gas.
    He had a few tricks like trace mineral mix
    So they'd weigh more comin' off grass.

Then the supplement salesman added
It all could be fed in his feed.
It showed on his graph that a pound and a half
Was expected, and Merlin agreed!

    The vet told me BVD cattle
    Gained less and I should vaccinate
    It was all Greek to me but HE had the degree
    And Lord knows I needed the weight!

Ear tags improved their performance
So I spent another big wad.
The message was clear, I put five in each ear
And even hung one on the cod!

    Then the implant peddlers attacked me!
    They convinced me my work wasn't done
    I had to agree so I used all three
    Heck, they even threw in a gun!

Then Alan Savory told me
What he'd learned out on the Savannah.
Ignoring expense, I bought enough fence
To hot wire the state of Montana!

    I wormed 'em, dehorned 'em and dipped 'em
    I sprayed 'em . . . hell, I did it all!
    Group therapy sessions, a priest for confessions
    And even a heifer on call!

So you see, I took ALL their advice!
I was baffled by brilliance galore.
And my steers did okay but I's hopin' that they
Would have weighed considerably more.

    'Cause if BS was measured in light bulbs
    My steers should have lit up the town
    And shown like a beacon, synergistically speakin'
    And weighed over two thousand pounds!"

THE VET'INARY'S LAUNDRY

There is nothing more disgusting,
More deserving to condemn
Than a basket full of laundry
From the local D.V.M.!

    See, afterbirth is oil base
    And needs to soak in hot
    Like adiposal tissue
    But blood, of course, is not.

It requires a frigid bath
To make the stain repent
Problem with cold water is
It sets the tag cement.

    While cat hair sneaks unnoticed
    Even by the sharpest eyer
    Then spreads like dying dandelions
    In contact with the dryer.

Samples long forgotten
In pockets pasted shut
Flavor all the laundry
With fermented porcine gut.

    Organophosphate fragrance
    Gently lingers in the air
    Mixing with the rumen contents
    On his underwear.

Iodine and methyl blue
Fetotomy remains
Dog shampoo, dehorning paste
And suppurating drains,.

Abscessed ears and hooves and horns
And poop from who knows what!
All gather in the dirty clothes
To spot and clot and rot,

And later gets recycled
As the ever present scum
That's now part of your Maytag
Living on ad nauseum.

    The vet'inary's laundry
    Can disrupt a married life.
    It's enough to make you jealous
    Of a truck mechanic's wife.

But there is no lofty moral
Just a sense of deja vu,
A warning now remembered,
That should have been a clue

    When your groom gave you his hanky
    As his darling bride-to-be,
    You should have been suspicious
    When it smelled like tomcat pee.

So don't let bloody coveralls
Or body parts of cows
Distract you from the promise
Spoken in your wedding vows.

    If laundry's come between you
    I'd suggest this little trick,
    Soak the spots in gasoline
    And flick it with your BIC!

POO BAH

I BELIEVE HE SAW ME COMIN'
HORSE TRADERS USUALLY DO
"I've got this chestnut gelding,
Might be just the horse for you.

Two trainers from Kentucky
Plan to look at him today.
I really shouldn't show him
But first come, first serve, I say.

He's the best I've got to offer
None better anywhere,"
THEN HE SAW ME EYE THE FILLY,
"Except, of course, that mare.

She's raced a million dirt tracks,
Everyone where I'm not barred,"
I RAISED A CROOKED EYEBROW
"Though, I never ran her hard.

She's as sound as Rockerfeller,
As healthy as ol' Shep,"
I FELT THE SCARS WHERE SHE'D BEEN NERVED,
"Precautionary step."

I RAN MY FINGERS DOWN HER LEG.
HER HOCKS WERE BIG AND SOFT.
"Mosquito bites, I reckon,
I'll throw in a can of Off."

SHE COUGHED AND RAISED A HEAVE LINE
THAT WOULD SCARE AN AUCTIONEER,
"The pollen count's been high this week,
Hay fever's bad this year.

I've priced her at a thousand bucks.
A bargain anyday
"But I'd consider half that much
If you took her today."

AS I STARTED FOR THE PICKUP
HE PLAYED HIS FINAL ACE,
"She's bred to Poo Bah's brother's son,
The finest stud to race."

I HELD MY NOSE TO SHOW HIM
POO BAH WASN'T DIDDLY SQUAT.
HE BLINKED AND QUICKLY ADDED
"But I don't believe she caught!"

FRECKLE'S ADVICE

Though Freckles is an angel now, he ain't forgot his friends.
He drops to earth and hangs around behind the buckin' pens.
He pulls a rope or just makes sure a rider gets bucked free
So I took it as an honor, the day he spoke to me . . .

"I saw you ride your bull today. You sure did yourself proud.
You had him by the short hairs, I could feel it in the crowd!"
"I really should be thankful that I even stayed aboard,
You could'a done it better, Freckles . . . I'm lucky that I scored!"

"Hey, don't be puttin' yourself down! You know you did okay.
The time will come when you'll look back and hunger for today
When everything was workin' right and judges liked your style,
Your joints were smooth, your belly flat and girls liked your smile.

'Cause in between the best you rode and the last one that you'll try
You'll face your own mortality and look it in the eye.
There ain't no shame admittin' you ain't what you used to be,
The shame is blamin' Lady Luck when Father Time's the key!

So if they know you came to ride and always did your best
Then hang your ol' spurs up with pride, 'cause that's the acid test
And, say some gunsel offers you a 'Geritol on Ice,'
Just grin'im down, 'cause you don't have to ride Tornado twice!"

RUNNIN' WILD HORSES

The chase, the chase, the race is on
The mustangs in the lead
The cowboys hot behind the band
Like centaurs, blurred with speed
    The horses' necks are ringin' wet
    From keepin' up the pace
    And tears cut tracks into the dust
    Upon the rider's face
The rank ol' mare sniffs out the trail
While never breakin' stride
But fast behind the wranglers come
Relentless, on they ride
    Until the canyon walls close in
    And punch'em through the gap
    Where bottled up, they paw and watch
    The cowboy shut the trap
And that's the way it's been out west
Since Cortez turned'em loose
We thinned the dinks and with the herd
We kept an easy truce
    But someone said they'd all die off
    If cowboys had their way
    So they outlawed runnin' horses
    But who am I to say
'Cause, hell, I'm gettin' older, boys
And though I miss the chase
His time, like mine, has come and gone
We're both so out of place
    The glamour of our way of life
    Belies our common fate
    I'm livin' off my pension check
    And he's a ward of state
But what a time! When he and I
Ran hard across the land
Me breathin' heavy down his neck
Him wearin' no man's brand
    No papers gave us ownership
    To all the ground we trod
    But it belonged to me and him
    As sure as there's a God
And if I could, I'd wish for him
And for myself, likewise
To finally cross the great divide
Away from pryin' eyes
    So in the end he has a chance
    To die with dignity
    His carcass laid to rest out there
    Where livin', he ran free
And coyotes chew his moldered bones
A fitting epilogue
Instead of smashed up in a can
For someone's townhouse dog.

THE FLAG

Ladies and gentlemen, I give you the flag
　　That flew over Valley Forge
Was torn in two by the gray and the blue
　　And bled through two world wars.

　　I give you the flag that burned in the street
　　　　In protest, in anger and shame,
　　The very same flag that covered the men
　　　　Who died defending her name.

　　　　We now stand together, Americans all,
　　　　　　Either by choice or by birth
　　　　To honor the flag that's flown on the moon
　　　　　　And changed the face of the earth.

　　　　　　History will show this flag stood a friend
　　　　　　　　To the hungry, the homeless and lost
　　　　　　That a mixture of men as common as clay
　　　　　　　　Valued one thing beyond cost.

　　　　　　　　And they've signed it in blood from Bunker Hill
　　　　　　　　　　To Saigon and Toko Ri.
　　　　　　　　I give you the flag that says to the world
　　　　　　　　　　Each man has a right to be free.

Don   baxter   Bob

"We thank y'all!"

ABOUT THE AUTHOR

cowboy poet, DVM and sorry team roper

COMMENTS

No one has ever accused my poetry of being up to Shakespeare's standards. But then Shakespeare never had to listen to a rancher's ramblings on the phone at 5:30 in the morning! People ask me where I get ideas for my poems. I tell 'em, "Look in the mirror!" The good Lord has furnished me with unlimited subject material. He plopped me down in the middle of the greatest show on earth, agriculture. So I muddle around in our world keeping an eye out for the prejudices and eccentricities that we take for granted.

My job is to turn over our sanctimonious stones and look at the holes in the queen's underwear. To gently locate our flaws and foibles and wrap them in hunter's flourescent orange. To nudge that fine line between good taste and throwing up in your hat. The livestock business generously offers up its participants as fodder.

Unfortunately, as is often the case, the peeing cow gets her own hocks wet! Nothing is more humbling than dealing with animals, cowboys or the weather.

I'm proud of this book. Donny and Bob turned out some of their best work. We hope you like it. 'Cause, after all, you are the reason we don't have real jobs!

I'm dedicating CROUTONS ON A COW PIE to one of the best men I've ever known. He always took time for us kids. He beat a living out of that Oklahoma red dirt for 80 years, paid his tithe, pulled his share of the load and told me the story behind the poem THE CONSULTANT . . . my Uncle Leonard.

BAXTER BLACK
Photo by Sue Rosoff

ABOUT THE ARTISTS

BOB BLACK

"He were a goofy lad," mused Bob's first grade teacher, Capt. Leep "Hardluck" Tudman, now-pilot of the salvage scow SS SNOOTS out of Port Arthur.

"I recalls fer 'show an' tell' he arranges t' have all th' other kids trucked to th' Alboma Copper Mine to spend th' day workin' th' pit. An fer 'parent's night' he drags in a badger an a racoon an refers to 'em lovin'ly all evenin' as "Mom" an "Dad."

"But I reckon th' real reason th' schoolboard decided to toss 'im in the open door of a passin' boxcar was his decision, fer 'is history project, to recreate the last great cattle drive over th' ol' Snub Trail usin' a hunnert an forty of his dad's rangy Herfords and 'er path lay straight through the principal's office."

The artist would like to thank his old teacher for those kind words and apologize to Mr. Ditz, the principal, if he's still around, for not realizing that he was an Angus man.

DON GILL

After a short bachelorhood Don has settled down with a beautiful wife, Denise. The art world has kept him busy, in both the serious and cartoon art. Don received the gold and bronze awards in the pen and ink divisions at last year's Western Art Roundup. Another boost to Don's serious art was the commission of twelve drawings by Spanish Springs Ranch in Northern California.

On the cartoon end, be looking for "Buck & Barney" two ol' cartoon cowboys that may be coming to your local paper.

Don would like to send a special thanks to his friends and especially his wife Denise, for their support.

COWBOY POETRY AVAILABLE BY BAXTER

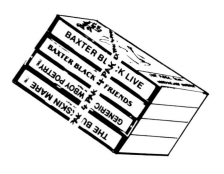

Coyote Cowboy Poetry © 1986

ISBN 0-939343-00-2

A 208-page hardback complete collection of Baxter's poetry written before his latest book, CROUTONS ON A COW PIE. It is fully illustrated by Don Gill, Bob Black and friends.

Some of the selections:

ONE MORE YEAR
SELLIN' PREWITT'S COW
THE COWBOY AND HIS DOG
FIVE FLAT
THE VEGETARIAN'S NIGHTMARE
THE COWBOY AND HIS TAPEWORM
COFFEE SHOP COMMUNION

THE COW COMMITTEE
LEGACY OF THE RODEO MAN
DOC, WHILE YER HERE
THE COYOTE
TAKE CARE OF YER FRIENDS
A RIDER, A ROPER AND A HELL'UVA WINDMILL MAN
OH NO, IT'S GONNA GO HIGHER!

and many more...

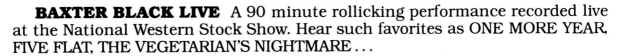

4 Pak Cassette Collection © 1987

A four cassette tape package of Baxter doing his own unique cowboy poetry, entitled:

BAXTER BLACK LIVE A 90 minute rollicking performance recorded live at the National Western Stock Show. Hear such favorites as ONE MORE YEAR, FIVE FLAT, THE VEGETARIAN'S NIGHTMARE...

BAXTER BLACK AND FRIENDS Baxter's poetry done by Baxter and some of his celebrity friends like Hoyt Axton, Red Steagall, Ed Bruce, Riders in the Sky, the Mystery Lady, and Walt Garrison, to name a few. Included are such poems as SUPERSALESMAN, A TIME TO STAY, THE COWBOY AND HIS DOG...

GENERIC COWBOY POETRY Recorded live at Bax's camp in Colorado complete with crackling fire, crickets and cowboy friends. Join them as Baxter does THE OYSTER, WHY DO THE TREES ALL LEAN IN WYOMING, THE SPUR and 15 more.

THE BUCKSKIN MARE Baxter's best selling cassette, to date. It is a chilling, touching collection of Bax's serious poetry. Like Edgar Allen Poe in spurs. Sure to send shivers up your spine. The title poem (15 minutes) is a story about one cowboy's obsession with a wild, invincible mustang. Not advised for people who think cowboys are frivolous and shallow. It includes RUNNIN' WILD HORSES, THE LOST DOG, GOODBYE OLD MAN...

"Baxter Black is not your normal poet."
DES MOINES REGISTER

ISBN 0-939343-03-7